CLASSIC COMMERCIAL VEHICLES

MALCOLM RANIERI

HALSGROVE

First published in Great Britain in 2011

British Library Cataloguing-in-Publication Data
A CIP record for this title is available from the British Library

ISBN 978 0 85704 093 0

HALSGROVE
Halsgrove House,
Ryelands Business Park,
Bagley Road, Wellington, Somerset TA21 9PZ
Tel: 01823 653777   Fax: 01823 216796
email: sales@halsgrove.com

Part of the Halsgrove group of companies.
Information on all Halsgrove titles is available at: www.halsgrove.com

Printed in China by Everbest Printing Co Ltd

INTRODUCTION

There was a time not too long ago when if you were to stand by a busy main road in Britain the majority of the commercial vehicles at work, whether they be vans, pick-ups, lorries of all types and emergency vehicles would all be manufactured in this country. Stand by the same main road in 2011 and it is unlikely that you will see anything like the same number of British-manufactured commercial vehicles at work, European makes, especially French, German and Swedish dominate.

The transport of raw materials and finished goods to and from factory, farm or shop to place of sale or consumer has always been a necessity throughout history. Up to the time of the Victorians the horse and water-borne carriers shouldered the burden of transport. During the nineteenth century, steam took over, as the railways expanded from the 1840s and moved people and goods, and traction engines appeared on the roads thirty years later, although canals still took their share of raw materials and goods, whilst the horse still contributed as it always had done. It has to be recognised that the roads of the period were not of a very high standard: in today's world they would be considered unsurfaced lanes, roughly surfaced with broken rocks or in the towns cobbles. Some toll and parish roads were reasonably maintained but these were the exceptions. They only improved after 1900 as motorised transport became readily available, and the invention of the steam road roller in late-Victorian times helped road construction and maintenance.

Commercial vehicles using the internal combustion engine have been around for about a century. It was during the late-Edwardian period prior to the First World War that the internal combustion engine and vehicle technology became refined enough to produce a commercial vehicle which would eventually supplant most other forms on the road. Steam had its last fling on the roads as the steam waggon or tractor was produced from around 1905: some examples continued working up to the Second World War and beyond, though apart from a few examples, manufacture ceased in the early-1930s. However, it was seen that the future lay in the use of the internal combustion engine, either petrol or diesel driven, and two-stroke as well as four-stroke; firms sprang up producing commercial vehicles all over Britain, including foreign firms like Ford and General Motors from the USA which opened factories in this country.

The early lorries were crude and unreliable, open cabs, no suspension, ineffective brakes, loads rarely exceeding 5 tons and average speeds below 12mph. The period from the First World War to the end of the twentieth century has seen a remarkable transformation in this form of transport, not always aided by legislation. Today's vehicles can carry loads of 30 tons or more, are ultra-reliable, having powerful engines and brakes, with state of the art cabs and average speeds undreamt of in the 1920s. Of course road conditions have improved tremendously over that period, A, B and minor roads have benefitted from surface improvements and highway control, and motorways were introduced in the second half of the twentieth century.

It is true to say that imported commercial vehicles have always been with us – in the early days French and German makes, some still extant, then between the World Wars USA makes were imported. Also for example the famous Bedford make was developed from the General Motors Chevrolet design, and Ford GB also benefitted from the parent company.

However, it is also true to say that in general British makes dominated the country's commercial transport system up to the last quarter of the twentieth century. Makes such as AEC, Albion, Bedford, ERF, Foden, Guy, Leyland, Scammell and Sentinel were the mainstay of the business. Gradually the industry suffered from the austerity period after the Second World War, industrial and labour problems, a dearth of new designs, foreign competition and take-overs and, like the car and motorcycle industries, British-built makes started to disappear from our roads.

Britain has always had a reputation for conserving its history, not just buildings and artifacts, but railways and steam engines, cars and motorcycles virtually anything which relates to its past. Commercial vehicles are no different. Individual enthusiasts, companies, museums and groups have preserved these vehicles for display and use for the last sixty years or so. One-make clubs have flourished, like the Leyland Society and the Sentinel Drivers Club, and general organisations like the Historic Commercial Vehicle Society (HCVS) set up in 1958, and the Commercial Vehicle & Road Transport Club (CVRTC), amongst others, look after the interests of owners and restorers, and promote general awareness of the movement. Museums have collections of commercial vehicles all over the country, some specialising in one particular make. The historic vehicles can also be seen on display at Steam Rallies and Shows, one-make gatherings, and road runs are organised on a local basis or under the control of organisations like the HCVS or the CTP (Commercial Transport in Preservation).

This book is illustrated with images of preserved commercial vehicles, buses and a few emergency vehicles, drawn only from the ranks of the British manufacturers, and the cut-off date is 25 years ago, though most examples are considerably older than that and a few date back to the First World War. The images are arranged loosely in alphabetical and chronological order to show where possible the advances made in production over the years. Military vehicles have not been included as that is a subject on its own. The images have been taken over a period of ten years or so and this collection is not meant to be comprehensive in coverage of British makes some makes have escaped my camera. I have tried apart from a few cases to avoid the steam rally or show line-up scenario and most images are taken on road runs or one-make events, stationary in an interesting environment, or on the road. It is without question impossible to recreate history so the images (whilst every effort has been taken to obtain authenticity) have been taken in modern conditions. The camera used has been a Mamiya 645, the medium format slides from 120 Fuji Velvia film having been scanned to produce a digital image.

Finally my admiration of those enthusiastic owners and restorers, who mostly at their own expense, work long hours in often difficult conditions to produce a pristine example of our commercial past, is boundless. I therefore dedicate this book to those enthusiasts with oily hands who create showroom condition from rusty wrecks, then allow people like myself to enjoy and photograph them in action. Long may it continue at 10 miles to the gallon.

Malcolm Ranieri

Opposite: AEC (The Associated Equipment Co. Ltd, of Southall, London-from 1927) 1948 Regal III Coach, Windover body, original company Trent number 611, in the attractive livery of Burton Coaches, in the company of an Austin Healey 3000 sports car and a Morris Minor saloon in a Somerset village.

AEC 1951 Matador 0853 Lorry, originally British Army as Tractor GS 10 ton Medium Artillery 4x4, disposed in 1968 and run as a breakdown vehicle for RJB Neale of Dagenham, later acquired by a farmer for general duties, entered preservation in 1986 and rebuilt in civilian style. The Matadors were all originally Forces vehicles, but their rugged build made them ideal general purpose vehicles when released from service. Photographed on the Historic Commercial Vehicle Society (HCVS), South Midlands, Ridgway Run at Quainton Road, Buckinghamshire.

Opposite: AEC 1954 Mammoth Major III Tipper Lorry photographed on the Ridgway Run at Quainton Road. The bridge carries the road over the railway line and the station terminus of the Buckinghamshire Railway Centre. This vehicle left the AEC Works as a six-wheeler, but was later converted by the factory to an eight-wheeler, operated from new by WJ King of Bishops Lydeard, Somerset, the road steam operator. It was in in derelict condition when found.

AEC 1958 Mercury Mark II Flatbed Lorry, photographed at the industrial site at Sharpness Docks, near Bristol, taking part in the 'Commercial Transport in Preservation' (CTP) Severn Valley and Cotswold Road Run, carrying a Fordson Tractor load. Bodied by Cravens Homalloy, it spent most of its working life in Lincolnshire delivering potatoes.

Opposite: AEC 1952 Regal IV Coach, Burlingham Seagull body, new to Scotts' Greys of Darlington and retired in the early-'60s, restored in the late-'70s and again in the mid-'90s. Seen here on the riverside of the River Thames at Henley on Thames.

AEC 1959 Mercury Lorry, seen at Lymm Services (Junction 20 of the M6 Motorway), at the start of the Cheshire Road Run, followed by an Albion Bus. New to Flowers Brewery, then Threlfalls in Liverpool.

AEC 1960 Mercury Horse Box, seen on the Cheshire Road Run on the A530 between Nantwich and Whitchurch, followed by an Atkinson Lorry.

AEC 1961 Reliance Bus, Willowbrook body, original company Western Welsh number 1284, seen at Blaenavon, South Wales. A Great Western Pannier Tank with a goods train passes over the bridge above on the Pontypool and Blaenavon Railway, as a Bedford Lorry overtakes the AEC. The Big Pit Mining Museum is located nearby.

AEC 1961 Routemaster Double Decker Bus, Park Royal body, the iconic London Transport 'Showbus', at Henley on Thames, taking part in the HCVS Ridgway Run.

Top left: AEC 1962 Mandator LWB (Long Wheel Base) Flatbed Lorry, at the Astwood Bank Steam Rally.

Top right: AEC 1968 Mercury Flatbed Lorry, entering the Lymm Services, at the start of the Cheshire Road Run.

Left: AEC 1971 Mercury Lorry, with a Nuffield Tractor load, on the Isle of Man during a break in a road run, near Douglas in the south of the island.

Opposite: ALBION 1915 Model A10 Lorry, 3 ton chain drive, one of 5560 purchased by the War Department for World War One, photographed near Jurby on the Isle of Man. Albion's factory was at Scotstoun, Glasgow. The emblem on the radiator of all Albions is a depiction of the rays of the sun, and the advertising slogan of this popular company was "Sure as Sunrise".

ALBION 1930 Type 26 Lorry, 5 litre engine, J. Lyons & Co. Ltd, near Jurby in the north of the Isle of Man.

Opposite: ALBION 1937 model CL Flatbed Lorry, at Dhoon Glen next to the station on the Manx Electric Railway, in the south of the Isle of Man, on a road run.

ALBION 1939 model FT3 Flatbed Lorry, photographed at Henley on Thames. This vehicle has a chequered work history. Registered in Birmingham, in early-1940 rebuilt by Chester Engineering and sold to Ex-Army Transport. Passed to North West Transport Service, then the brewers Taylor Walker of London, again to brewers Ind Coope of Burton on Trent, and (somewhat of a come down) ended its working life as a coal lorry in Derbyshire. Restored twenty years ago.

Opposite: ALBION 1935 model LB4 Lorry, originally a Post Office Telephone Linesman Van in Brecon, photographed at Wentnor, in the county of Shropshire.

ALBION 1939 Type 26 Lorry, spent all its working life as a Shell Mex and BP carrier of 300 2-gallon oil cans, photographed near Jurby in the north of the Isle of Man.

19

ALBION 1950 model FT35 Clansman Lorry. Note the 'Explosives' warning sign on the radiator which must have been its load at some time in its working history. Seen at Lymm Services, at the start of the Cheshire Road Run.

ALBION 1950, another FT35 Clansman. This time the Flatbed Lorry version, demonstrating one of the variations of the same model as in the previous picture, which could be ordered new or rebuilt. Also at Lymm Services.

ALBION 1955 model MLH 3N Cairn Flatbed Lorry, a rare example, at the Prees Heath Truck Stop, Shropshire.

ALBION 1955 model MR9 Nimbus Bus, Scottish Omnibus body. This was one of the factory demonstrators, now painted in Berresfords company red livery, at Lymm Services.

Opposite: ALBION 1956 model Chieftan Flatbed Lorry, on a road run approaching Ramsey on the Isle of Man.

ALBION 1966 model Reiver Flatbed Lorry, at the Onslow Park Steam Rally.

Opposite: ALBION 1970 model Reiver Lorry, showing the difference a few years makes in the model, and the same haulage company Albert Davies of Acton Burnell. Photographed on the Heart of Wales Road Run at Marton on the B4386 in Shropshire.

ATKINSON 1968 model Raider Lorry, photographed at Butterley on the HCVS Derbyshire Limestone Road Run, opposite the Midland Railway Centre, the destination of the run. Atkinsons were manufactured in Preston and started with steam in 1916: one steam wagon is preserved in this country.

Opposite: ALVIS 1948 model TA14 Shooting Brake or Woody, bodied by Guests, at Point of Ayre Lighthouse in the north of the Isle of Man. These Shooting Brakes or Estate Cars were regularly used for the transport of small goods working mainly for shop owners or small businesses. Alvis was based at Coventry in the Midlands.

ATKINSON 1970s' model Borderer Recovery Vehicle, outside the former Butterley Iron Works, on the HCVS Derbyshire Limestone Road Run, with another Atkinson in the background.

AUSTIN 1937 10/4 Shooting Brake, a rare survivor of the chrome radiatored vans, photographed at Sharpness Docks at the start of the CTP Severn Valley and Cotswold Road Run, with the Social Club building in the background. The Austin Motor Co. Ltd were manufacturers at Longbridge, Birmingham.

AUSTIN 1940s' model K4 NFS Turntable Ladder Vehicle. The National Fire Service was created in Great Britain in 1941, an amalgamation of the Auxiliary Fire Service (APS) and the then Local Authority Fire Brigades. It existed until 1948, disbanded by the Fire Services Act, 1947, when control reverted to Local Authorities again. Photographed at the Kemble Rally held on the airfield, a redundant hangar forming the background.

Opposite: AUSTIN 1939 Ruby Van, appropriately with Austin Village, Longbridge legend signwritten on the side. Photographed at Astwood Bank Steam Rally, with part of the Davis family's collection of earth moving equipment in the background.

AUSTIN 1948 model K8 Welfarer Ambulance, a rare model, photographed outside Bewdley Station, Severn Valley Railway.

Opposite: AUSTIN 1952 model K4 Loadstar, photographed in the village of Pebworth, Worcestershire – appropriate as these vehicles were used extensively in the Vale of Evesham for carrying produce.

AUSTIN 1962 model FFK140, at Lymm Services, at the start of the Cheshire Road Run.

AUSTIN 1950 model A40 Pick-Up, at Evesham Vale Truck Stop, Worcestershire. Appropriately an ex-Austin Service vehicle, this type of vehicle was very popular with farmers and small businesses: produce, livestock and small engineering goods could be carried with ease at a relatively low cost compared to a lorry.

BEDFORD 1932 model W5 Fish and Chip Van. The actual body was originally on a donkey cart, then a Model T Ford. In 1932 the body was swapped onto the Bedford frame by a village blacksmith, and used for selling fish and chips into the 1950s. Photographed at Marlow on the HCVS South Midlands Ridgway Run. Bedfords were manufactured in Luton as part of Vauxhall Motors, which in turn was part of General Motors.

BEDFORD 1938 model BYC Light Lorry. This vehicle was supplied by Geo. Clarke & Sons to Burrows of Stratford upon Avon, Warwickshire, and built to carry sheep and deliver market garden produce to Coventry Market seen at Henley on Thames at the start of the HCVS South Midlands Ridgway Run.

BEDFORD 1946 O Type Artic Lorry, this vehicle was operated by Vantona Textiles until 1953, purchased by Geo. Clarke & Sons of Alcester, Warwickshire and fitted with a breakdown body and crane. Fully restored in 1986 to its original body and livery, it is shown here on the approaches to Marlow on the HVCS South Midlands Ridgway Run.

Clockwise from top left: BEDFORD 1949 model OLB, originally a RAF Tanker, restored as a Flatbed Lorry, and photographed at the Astwood Bank Steam Rally; BEDFORD 1949 model OJ Tpper Lorry, originally an Isle of Man lorry carrying sand and gravel, restored in the livery of Elliots of Cheltenham in the same business, at the Astwood Bank Steam Rally; BEDFORD 1953 model A3 Horse Box, a rare model, laid in a barn from 1967 to 2002, restored to run on LPG fuel, at Blaenavon, South Wales; BEDFORD 1950 O Type Lorry, typical of thousands used in haulage in the '50s and '60s, at Henley on Thames.

BEDFORD 1953 O Type Flatbed Lorry, used extensively in the market gardens in the Vale of Evesham, here appropriately at Pebworth Nurseries, Worcestershire.

BEDFORD 1955 S Type Lorry (note tied tarpaulin cover over the goods), photographed outside Toddington Station, headquarters of the Gloucestershire Warwickshire Railway.

BEDFORD 1950s' J Type Tipper Lorry, photographed at St John's on the Isle of Man on a road run.

BEDFORD OB Coaches photographed at night at the Kemble Steam Rally outside one of the redundant aircraft hangars. Note the 1949 Metropolitan Police version.

Opposite: BEDFORD 1950 OB Type Coach, the iconic people carrier of the '40s and '50s, here in IOM Coaches light blue livery (note registration number), alongside the Manx Electric Railway Toastrack Tramcar number 33, and photographed above Douglas, Isle of Man.

BEDFORD 1950s' OXC Type Timber Tractor, 28hp 3.5 litre straight six engine, photographed on a Somerset farm near Taunton.

BEDFORD 1957 A Type Dropside Lorry, at the Kemble Steam Rally outside one of the redundant aircraft hangars.

BEDFORD 1960 TJ Type Tipper Lorry, with the tipper in action, at the Bowes Railway, Gateshead, Tyne and Wear.

45

BEDFORD 1966 S Type Side Tipper Lorry, at Lymm Services at the start of the Cheshire Road Run.

BEDFORD 1971 KM Type Tractor Unit, photographed at Marton village at the start of the Heart of Wales Road Run.

BMC (British Motor Corporation) 1968 FC Type Flatbed Lorry, with the colloquially named "Threepenny Cab", crossing the swing bridge at Sharpness Docks on the CTP Severn Valley and Cotswold Road Run. BMC was the name adopted on the merger of Austin and Morris in 1952. Other well-known firms were amalgamated later such as Guy and Coventry Climax, and finally in 1968 Leyland to form British Leyland Motor Corporation.

BMMO (Birmingham and Midland Motor Omnibus Company Ltd) 1965 Double Decker Bus, self-built by the bus company, photographed in the town of Alcester, Warwickshire.

BRISTOL 1950 L5G Bus (Half -Cab), ECW (Eastern Coach Works) body, originally a Crossville, North Wales bus number KG131, here near Ash Priors in Somerset, in the company of a Morris Minor car and a Bedford OXC Timber Tractor (see page 44). The Bristol Tramway & Carriage Co. was of course located in Bristol.

BRISTOL 1955 HG6L Flatbed Lorry, here climbing the notorious Fish Hill on the A44 near Broadway, Worcestershire, a difficult ascent or descent before the days of powerful engines and brakes on commercial vehicles. This BRS (British Road Services) vehicle worked out of Cheapside, Birmingham Depot.

BRISTOL HG6Ls Flatbed BRS Lorries, from left to right, built in 1953, 1957 and 1955, at a farm in Birlingham, Vale of Evesham, Worcestershire. Note the sheeted and tied tarpaulin covers.

Clockwise from top left: BRISTOL 1961 HA6LL Artic Flatbed Lorry, photographed at Lincoln Farm Café, near Balsall Common, at a BRS (British Road Services) gathering: this particular vehicle was based at Oldbury, Black Country, Depot; COMMER 1934 Centaur Coach, photographed near Nantwich on the Cheshire Road Run: Commer Cars Ltd were based in Luton; COMMER 1961 model CDTS3, one previous owner when purchased from a scrapyard in a very sorry state, a complete restoration to a very high standard followed, and seen here at the riverside in Henley on Thames, at the start of the HCVS South Midlands Ridgway Run; COMMER 1970 Maxi Load, photographed at the start of the CTP Severn Valley and Cotswold Road Run.

DOUGLAS (of Cheltenham) Equipment Ltd, 1950s' Timber Tractor, built from parts supplied by AEC. Basically a Matador vehicle, shown here at Inkberrow, Worcestershire, with the current owner's, Living Van attached.

DAIMLER 1920s' Worthington Advertising Vehicle, part of the Burton on Trent Brewing Museum collection, actually fitted with a Bedford engine, seen at Winchcombe Station on the Gloucestershire Warwickshire Railway. Daimlers were manufactured in Coventry.

DAIMLER 1948 CVD6SD, Burlingham body, original company Alexander number D19, photographed at Marlow, on the HCVS South Midlands Ridgway Run.

Opposite: DAIMLER 1939 COG5-40, Willowbrook body, original company Tailby & George, Willington number DR5, photographed in Somerset next to an original Somerset County Council road sign.

DAIMLER 1949 CVD6SD, Weymann body, original company Exeter number 73, photographed at Bewdley, Worcestershire.

DENNIS 1925 G Type,15 ton payload, spent its working life in New Zealand, now residing on the Isle of Man where the picture was taken. Dennis Bros Ltd were a Guildford, Surrey firm.

Opposite: DENNIS 1956 model Falcon II Single Decker Bus, 30 seat Strachan body, original company Aldershot and District number 282, here at Henley on Thames.

DENNIS 1956 model Horla Tractor Unit, a rare vehicle, part of the Bowmans Museum collection, here photographed outside Timothy Hackworth's house (railway pioneer), Shildon in the North East.

DENNIS 1958 5 ton Flatbed Lorry, in the original livery of Whitbread Brewery Co. which it carried in its working life, photographed at Henley on Thames.

DENNIS 1950s' model Max Flatbed Lorry, photographed at the Bedfordshire Steam Rally in the grounds of Shuttleworth House.

Opposite: DENNIS 1959 Flatbed Lorry, in the livery of Marshalls Transport of Evesham, pictured here at Davis's Yard, Astwood Bank, Worcestershire, on the occasion of the Steam Rally.

DODGE 1958 model 3145 Flatbed Lorry, photographed at Dhoon Glen, Isle of Man, next to the Manx Electric Railway station, taking part in a road run. Dodge Bros (GB) Ltd were situated in Park Royal, London.

DODGE 1974 model 500 Tractor Unit, here photographed at rest near Douglas, Isle of Man.

DODGE 1983 model Commando 2 Flatbed Lorry, here at Quainton Road, Buckinghamshire, taking part in the Ridgway Run.

ERF (E R Foden Ltd) 1943 model C15 Lorry, one of the vehicles of the former works fleet of engine makers L. Gardner & Sons of Patricroft, Manchester, purchased direct by the current owner from that famous company. Photographed at Butterley opposite the Midland Railway Centre, having taken part in the Derbyshire Limestone Road Run. ERF were manufactured at Sandbach, Cheshire.

Opposite: ERF 1957 model KV Lorry taking part in the CTP Severn Valley and Cotswold Road Run, which started at Sharpness Docks and took a circular route through the South Cotswolds, here running through the attractive Cotswold town setting of Painswick on the A46, in the livery of Hodgsons of Carlisle.

ERF 1966 Six-wheeled Luton Van, in the livery of Lawleys, China and Glass Specialists, departing the Prees Heath Truck Stop in Shropshire on the Cheshire Road Run. This vehicle was new to William Boulton of Stone as a flatbed, the Luton body was built as a display unit for Royal Doulton in the livery of Lawleys. It was then used by a circus and toured all over Europe. It has now been returned to the Lawleys livery.

Opposite: ERF 1963 model KV Lorry, in the livery of Vic Haines of Pershore in whose hands the vehicle remains, here at Winchcombe Station on the Gloucestershire Warwickshire Railway seen in the background.

ERF 1969 model LV Tanker Lorry, in the striking orange livery of Rugby Cement, here on the Thames riverside at Henley on Thames.

ERF 1970 Tractor Unit. Two forms of haulage with half a century of progress between them meet at the Chilterns Steam Rally, the ERF standing next to a 1921 Garrett 4CD Steam Tractor.

ERF 1971 model 54G Flatbed Lorry, here photographed with farm buildings in the background at Birlingham in the Vale of Evesham, Worcestershire.

Opposite: ERF 1970 Cattle Truck, on the road on the Cheshire Road Run between Nantwich and Whitchurch. The vehicle was new in 1970 as a Flatbed Lorry, but stored and only registered in 1986 as a Cattle Truck, hence the registration number.

ERF 1973 model A Series Artic, an Eastern BRS vehicle which was based at Newark Depot, here at a BRS gathering at Lincoln Farm Café, Balsall Common.

FODEN 1925 Steam Waggon called "Superior" with a Sentinel Tar Sprayer behind, taking part in a road run at Edgerley in Shropshire, passing Rookery Farm. Fodens were manufactured at Sandbach, Cheshire.

Opposite: FODEN Steamers raising steam at Beaulieu Abbey in the New Forest on the occasion of the Steam Rally held in the grounds. On the left is a 1927 Waggon called "Sir Ector" and on the right is a 1929 Waggon called "Roby"; another Foden Steamer can be seen in the background.

FODEN 1927 Steam Tractor photographed in front of the gatehouse to Eastnor Castle, Herefordshire, on the occasion of the September Steam Party. This vehicle is part of the collection at the castle.

FODEN 1928 Steam Tractor, with its trailer attached and photographed in the grounds of Beaulieu Abbey.

FODEN 1930 Steam Waggon, in the livery of Mechanical Tar Spraying and Grouting Ltd, photographed outside Shuttleworth House, Bedfordshire, on the occasion of the Bedfordshire Steam Rally. A number of Fodens (and Sentinels) were converted to tar spraying vehicles at the end of their working life. Steam manufacture came to an end in the early-1930s and Fodens then built diesel lorries.

Opposite: FODEN 1934 S Type Lorry and Trailer, photographed crossing Castlemorton Common, near Malvern, Worcestershire, going home from the Welland Steam Rally. It is one of the oldest Foden diesel lorries in existence.

FODEN 1949 model S18 Lorry, photographed at Marton village on the Heart of Wales Road Run.

Opposite: FODEN 1945 model DG6/10 Timber Tractor, built for the Ministry of Defence as a 10 ton gun tractor, demobbed in 1944 and converted into a timber tractor, here at St John's in the Isle of Man on a road run.

FODEN 1950 model FG61S 8-wheeler Flatbed Lorry, here at Quainton Road on the Ridgway Run.

FODEN 1958 model S20 Artic Lorry. This 2-stroke unit was new to Esso and used for fuel deliveries, then to F. & A. Nixon of Birmingham, discovered in a quarry at Brownhills together with the York tipping trailer and restored. Photographed entering the Commercial Vehicle & Road Transport Club (CVRTC) Gaydon Classic Commercial Vehicle Show.

FODEN 1959 model S20 Tipper Lorry, in its original livery of the Breedon & Cloud Hill Lime Works, photographed at Butterley, Derbyshire.

FODEN 1967 model S34 Flatbed Lorry, in its original Shipstone Brewery, Nottingham fleet livery, complete with a part-load of beer barrels, photographed at Marlow on the Ridgway Run.

FODEN 1967 model S20 Tipper Lorry, with its tipper engaged, photographed at Butterley, Derbyshire.

FORD 1916 model T Convertible, Ford's everyman vehicle which revolutionised transport, photographed at Jurby in the Isle of Man. Ford is a Dagenham, Essex firm.

Opposite: FORD 1932 model A 1 ton Truck, photographed at the Black Country Living Museum on the quayside of the arm of the Dudley Canal which is part of the museum. Behind the vehicle is a canal tugboat used as an ice breaker.

FORD 1929 model AA 1 ton Truck, photographed at night at the Kemble Rally, with a redundant aircraft hangar in the background.

Opposite: FORDSON 1945 5cwt Van, unloading luggage outside Bewdley Station on the Severn Valley Railway.

FORDSON 1946 model 7V Artic Lorry, photographed at Gaydon Classic Commercial Motor Show.

Opposite: FORD 1961 Thames Trader Lorry, new to N Painting, a Berkshire general haulage firm at work carrying sand and gravel up to the late-'80s, before entering preservation. Photographed at Henley on Thames.

FORDSON 1949 Thames ET6 Recovery Vehicle, photographed at Marlow on the Ridgway Run.

FORD 1964 Thames Trader Vehicle Transporter, showing the variations available on certain models from makers, here entering Marlow, passing the Hare and Hounds public house.

FORD 1967 model D800 Tractor Unit and Trailer, on the road between Nantwich and Whitchurch on the Cheshire Road Run.

FORD 1970/3 model D1000 Recovery Vehicles photographed at Lymm Services.

Opposite: FOSTER 1921 Steam Waggon called "Sir William Tritton". Very few of these waggons built at Lincoln are preserved, this particular one coming from New South Wales, Australia. Photographed at the Banbury Steam Rally, Oxfordshire.

GUY 1948 Wolf Bus, Barnard body, original company Llandudno, here seen passing a line-up of Bedford OBs at the Kemble Steam Rally. Guys were manufactured in Wolverhampton.

Opposite: GARRETT 1926 class QL Steam Waggon. This Leiston, Suffolk-built vehicle, is photographed with Shuttleworth House in the background, at the Bedfordshire Steam Rally.

GUY 1950 Wolf Bus, Ormac body, original company McConnacher, Ballaculish, Scotland, here running round the internal roads of the Black Country Living Museum and passing the Tram Shed, appropriate as these vehicles were built at Wolverhampton.

Opposite: GUY 1949 Wolf Parcel Van, photographed outside the old weighbridge office at the colliery of the Black Country Living Museum. The John Lewis Partnership operated an extensive fleet of delivery vehicles, this particular one working in the West End, London.

GUY 1950s' Otter Flatbed Lorry, here at Lymm Services at the start of the Cheshire Road Run.

Opposite: GUY 1953 Special Bus, Eastern Carriage Works body, original London Transport number 326, passing the tram lines at the Black Country Living Museum.

GUY 1958 Vixen Furniture Van, in the famous livery of the Pickfords Removals firm, photographed at the BRS gathering at Lincoln Farm Café, Balsall Common.

JENSEN 1954 Flatbed Lorry, at the Evesham Vale Truck Stop, Worcestershire.

Opposite: JENSEN 1951 model JLC 6 ton Flatbed Lorry, another Black Country firm better known for their sports cars, passing the Tram Shed at the Black Country Living Museum. Jensen Motors Ltd were based at West Bromwich.

JOWETT 1947 Bradford Light Lorry, photographed at Crich Tram Museum, Derbyshire. Behind is Liverpool Corporation Tram number 869 built in 1936, and a selection of British-built cars, MG, Morris, etc. Jowett Cars Ltd were built at Bradford, Yorkshire, hence the model name.

LEYLAND. The Mike Sutcliffe, MBE collection of superbly restored historic vehicles was photographed at Crich Tramway Museum, the oldest being (on the right) 1913 Leyland model S3 Birch 36 seat Open Double Decker Omnibus and (on the left) 1905 Leyland model X Tilling 34 seat Open Double Decker Omnibus. The next four images are all part of the collection. Leyland Motors Ltd manufactured vehicles in Preston, Lancashire, and also made steam wagons in the early days, three of which are preserved in this country.

LEYLAND 1914 model S4 36hp 32 seat Torpedo Charabanc in the livery of the London North Western Railway.

Top left: LEYLAND 1921 model S19/5 30hp Dodson 32 seat Convertible Charabus.

Top right: LEYLAND 1923 model SG7 36hp 40 seat Saloon Single Decker Omnibus in the stunning livery of the White Rose Motor Buses Company, North Wales. Some recreation actors in period clothing stand next to the vehicle.

Left: LEYLAND 1924 model L85 S.19 Dodson 48 seat Double Decker Omnibus, called the "Chocolate Express", which worked in London.

Opposite: LEYLAND 1929 model LTB1 Lioness Charabanc, photographed at Chatham Docks, Kent, in company with a Barclay steam industrial locomotive, a portable steam engine and steam cranes in the background.

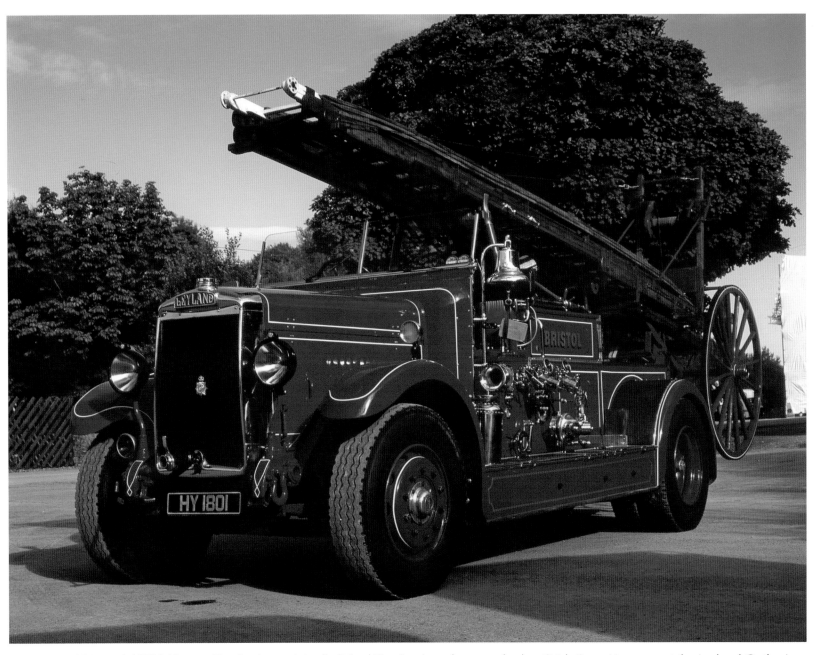

LEYLAND 1931 model LTB1 Lioness Fire Engine, originally Bristol Fire Service, photographed at Crich Tram Museum, at the Leyland Gathering.

LEYLAND 1932 model TA4 Badger Flatbed Lorry, at Crich Tramway Museum.

LEYLAND 1948 Beaver Flatbed Lorry, originally a National Health Service Mass X-Ray Unit in the Birmingham area until the late-'60s, preserved as a flatbed, photographed at Henley on Thames.

LEYLAND 1950 model ECO/ 1R Comet Flatbed Lorry, photographed at Crich Tramway Museum.

LEYLAND 1952 model PS2/12A Tiger Single Decker Bus photographed at night at Crich Tramway Musem. The tram is a 1925 Leeds number 399.

LEYLAND 1968 model PD3/11 Titan Double Decker Bus, Metro-Cammell-Weymann body, originally Blackpool number 529, Taken at night at Heaton Park Tramway, Manchester, on the occasion of their Blackpool weekend, hence the company of Blackpool Balloon Tram number 706.

Opposite: LEYLAND 1957 Comet Artic Flatbed Lorry, in BRS livery and worked from the Norwich Depot, photographed at Lincoln Farm Café, Balsall Common.

LEYLAND 1970 model FBF457H Super Comet Lorry, photographed at Onslow Park Steam Rally. Behind is a 1958 Dodge.

LEYLAND 1970 model 16LBT/19BR Badger Flatbed Lorry, photographed at Spiers and Hartwell's Honeybourne, Worcestershire Depot, in company with a current fleet Scania Lorry.

MAUDSLAY 1948 Mogul II Flatbed Lorry, here in Marton village on the Heart of Wales Road Run. The Maudslay Motor Co Ltd originally hailed from Coventry.

Opposite: MANN 1919 Steam Waggon, in the livery of Beyer, Peacock & Co. Ltd, Manchester, steam railway engine builders to the world. Mann Patent Steam Cart & Wagon Co. Ltd was a Leeds company. The photograph was taken at Astwood Bank, Worcestershire.

MORRIS 1958 model JB Commercial Light Tipper, a rare vehicle, here with the tipper in action at Bewdley Station, Severn Valley Railway.

Opposite: MORRIS 1924 Snub Nose Light Van, a rare example of an early Morris commercial vehicle. The tram is a 1922 Glasgow number 22, here at Crich Tramway Museum. Morris Motors Ltd were situated in Cowley, Oxford; Morris Commercial Cars Ltd took over the old Wolseley Works in Adderley Park, Birmingham from 1933.

MORRIS 1960 model LC5 Commercial Light Lorry, here at Davis's Yard, Astwood Bank, Worcestershire, with a Garrett Traction Engine in the background, and modern earth moving equipment.

MORRIS 1960 Mini Van, operated by Post Office Telephones. The Mini was a revolutionary design in the 1950s and was adapted for all sorts of commercial requirements including Police Patrol Vans. Here photographed in a Somerset village.

Opposite: RELIANT 1949 Girder Fork Van. These were used for local deliveries especially for the Co-Operative. Seen here in company with a 1935 Morris 10/4 Special Coupe car at the Black Country Living Museum. Reliant built at Tamworth and are justly famous for their three-wheeler cars and vans.

SCAMMELL 1937 model MH3 Mechanical Horse. These were used extensively on the railways for local deliveries, and fittingly the MH3 is pictured at Bewdley Station, Severn Valley Railway. Other later three-wheel models were called Scarab and Townsman. Scammells were built at Watford, and seemed to aim for each end of the commercial market from the small three-wheelers to enormous heavy haulage vehicles.

Opposite: ROWE 1958 Hillmaster, built by a small manufacturer (and coach operator) at Doublebois, Cornwall, from 1953 to 1962. Here it is pictured at Colerne Airfield, on the CTP Bournemouth to Colerne Road Run.

SCAMMELL 1952 model 15MU Tractor Unit. This vehicle was a brewery vehicle which then worked for Len Firborough of Leicester on showgrounds attached to a "Big Wheel". It is in company with 1949 Barclay Steam Railway Engine which worked for the NCB (National Coal Board), pictured at the Bowes Railway, Gateshead, Tyne and Wear.

Opposite: SCAMMELL 1946 Showtrac, used on the fairgrounds where in some cases it replaced the steam engine Showman's which hauled fairground equipment between venues and then powered the lights or the rides. Here fittingly the Showtrac is pictured in front of the 1890s' Gallopers at the Chilterns Steam Rally.

SCAMMELLS line-up. Four fairground engines from the '50s/'60s are seen at the Recreation Ground, Stratford upon Avon, Warwickshire, having attended an Old Tyme Fair on the town's Recreation Ground next to the River Avon. R. Edwards were an old established fairground operator from Swindon.

SCAMMELL 1971 Trunker Tanker Lorry, here pictured at Lymm Services.

SEDDON ATKINSON 1950s' Flatbed Lorry, still under restoration for Allelys Transport, Studley, Warwickshire, when photographed at Astwood Bank. The firm was an amalgamation of two firms as the name implies, with Seddon based at Salford.

Opposite: SEDDON ATKINSON 1960 model 15/10/375 Flatbed Lorry, seen on the road near Gaydon in Warwickshire. Originally with S Gardner & Son of Gloucester. Also used on haulage in the West Country and South Wales, later with Alexander Lyon a Bedfordshire showman, entered preservation in 1987 and in original livery.

SENTINEL. Two Steam Waggons, a 1920 Standard Waggon and on the right a 1924 Super Waggon, pictured outside Shuttleworth House. Sentinels began life as Alley and Maclellan of Polmadie, Glasgow and commenced steam waggon (always spelt with two gs) production in 1905; due to a company buy-out the company relocated to the famous Sentinel Works in Shrewsbury in 1915.

SENTINEL 1926 Super Steam Tractor 2 speed, this rare vehicle came from Australia and was restored in this country. Photographed at Belvoir Castle Steam Rally, Leicestershire.

SENTINEL 1929 model DG4 Steam Waggon Tar Sprayer, originally Erdington Haulage to 1942, then various contractors to 1968 when bought by Lloyd-Jones Bros as a Tar Sprayer, the livery it now carries. Photographed at Edgerley, Shropshire on a road run.

SENTINEL 1931 model DG4P Steam Waggon, carrying the livery of Morris Oils (or Lubricants as they are now known) a famous old Shrewsbury firm, in company with at the time (2004) modern haulage Scania Lorry in current livery, but also another vehicle in the early green livery, a 1928 Ford model AA. Photographed in the factory yard. Behind the vehicles is the former London North Western Railway Goods Shed. The Sentinel was new to Samuel Banner & Co of Bootle.

Opposite: SENTINEL 1935 model S4 Steam Waggon, new to Price & Co, Bakers Ltd of Forest Gate, Essex, here carrying the livery of the brewers Shepherd Neame of Faversham, and pictured at Chatham Docks in the company of a steam portable and steam cranes.

SENTINEL 1936 model DG4 Tractor Unit (on the right), in company with a diesel Sentinel Flatbed Lorry from 1955 (a DV4/4), pictured in the remains of the Sentinel Works at Shrewsbury. The steam vehicle was new to Mickleover Transport, Chard, Somerset, then back to the Sentinel Works in 1942, eventually passing to the well-known steam contractor Richard Woolley of Bucknell, Shropshire in 1953; the diesel lorry was a Wilsons Brewery vehicle.

SENTINEL 1955 model DV4/4 Flatbed Lorry, originally operated by Booths Steel of Bolton, followed into Lymm Services by a Morris.

SENTINEL 1953 model DV4/4 Lorry, originally owned by Sir Lindsay Parkinson, photographed at Edgerley, Shropshire.

Opposite: TILLING-STEVENS 1949 model K6LA7Single Decker Bus, Scottish Aviation body, operated by Warrens of Alton, photographed in the company of an Austin Healey 3000 at Great Alne Village Hall, Warwickshire. Great Alne was home to a Maudslay Motors factory from the 1940s, now closed. Tilling-Stevens factory was in Maidstone, Kent.

THORNEYCROFT 1945 Sturdy Flatbed Lorry, supplied new to Wethereds Brewery of Marlow to 1962, then to a haulier in Emsworth; up to 1965 it worked as a coal lorry for Sibleys Coal Merchants of Rownham, Southampton, and rescued for preservation from a scrapyard in 1996. Thorneycroft hailed from Basingstoke, and also made steam waggons in the early 1900s, three of which are preserved in this country.

THORNEYCROFT 1948 Sturdy Flatbed Lorry, photographed at night in the company of a 1918 Ruston and Hornsby Steam Tractor at Llanfair Caereinion Station on the Welshpool to Llanfair narrow gauge railway in the county of Powys, Wales.

YORKSHIRE 1905 Steam Waggon, called "Denby Maiden", pictured at the Lincoln Steam Rally. The Yorkshire Patent Steam Wagon Co Ltd was located in Leeds.

Opposite: THORNEYCROFT 1961 Swiftsure Flatbed Lorry, carrying barrels of Stone Ales, and pictured at Belvoir Castle, Leicestershire.

YORKSHIRE 1927 class WG Steam Waggon, called "Yorkshire Lad". It is interesting to compare this and the previous vehicle of 1905, at the start of production and 22 years later towards the end. Photographed at the Welland Steam Rally, Worcestershire.

Opposite: The bane of the delivery man holding up his progress, but essential to the well-being of our road infrastructure, the road making gang. Here a demonstration gang, often seen at rallies, are working on a piece of private road, but next to the minor road which goes to Ash Priors in Somerset. On the road can be seen a 1950 Albion Clansman. Their clothes and equipment would suggest some time in 1940s or early-1950s.

To finish this look at our commercial heritage I have included an image of road versus rail, but only as a demonstration of what may have occurred in the past at the docks and still does in certain areas. Often rail complemented the road haulage, the steam engine bringing the off-loaded goods from the sea-going vessel to the pick-up points for the lorries to distribute. The steam engine is a Lancashire & Yorkshire (British Railways logo) 1891-built 0-4-0 Saddle Tank, number 51222 (actually 51218), a dock shunter known as a "Pug". On either side of the loco-motive is a Fordson 7V and a Leyland Octopus, and the dock is at Goole, East Riding of Yorkshire.